G000060858

Ann Ward was born in Listowel and lived in Ballyduff until her family moved to Galway. She was educated in Dominican College, Taylor's Hill. Ann then worked in Germany and later returned to Ireland and she worked in Clonmel and Kanturk. Ann now lives in Mallow with her husband James and two children. She gives courses on microwave cookery throughout the country together with training courses for electrical sales people and private groups.

THE IRISH MICROWAVE COOK BOOK

ANN WARD

MERCIER PRESS

Mercier Press,
PO Box 5, 5 French Church Street, Cork
16 Hume Street, Dublin 2

© Ann Ward 1993

ISBN 1 85635 069 X

1 0   9   8   7   6

To my husband James and children Laura and Brian whose patience and judgment helped me greatly in the research for this book.
For Eugene, Sheila and Hugh.

This book is sold subject to the condition that it shall not, by way of trade or otherwise, be lent, resold, hired out or otherwise circulated without the publisher's prior consent in any form of binding or cover other than that in which it is published and without a similar condition including this condition being imposed on the subsequent purchaser.

Printed in Ireland by Colour Books

Contents

Fish   63

Introduction

Microwave cookers now play a very important role in the kitchen. They are faster, more economical and healthier. They cut down on the amount of time spent in the kitchen to allow the cook more free time to pursue other activities.

Microwave cookers have been in America for thirty years, so they are no newcomers to the kitchen. Here, however, they are relatively new. As with all new appliances, instruction is very important. I have found after microwave cookery demonstrations that people have requested my recipes and advice. They have written to me to know if I intended writing a cookery book. Here it is.

As with my cookery demonstrations, I concentrate on everyday recipes which anyone can use. I have tried to keep these recipes very basic and hope my readers will have the ingredients already on their weekly shopping list.

All the recipes here are based on a 700 watt oven but please remember that ovens vary as do the shape and size of the items cooked and therefore you may need to alter your timing to suit.

The Irish Microwave Cookbook is also for those of you who only use your microwave for reheating and defrosting. Now you can try each and every one of the following recipes as you cannot go wrong with them.

I will look forward to meeting my readers at various locations throughout the country when I am giving cookery demonstrations.

ANN WARD

Dear Reader,

Sanyo Ireland are delighted to be involved with Ann Ward and the Mercier Press in the production of this book. We chose this particular partnership because it's the first time we've come across a book with a truly commonsense approach. It gives recipes for dishes that are a regular part of everyday life in Irish homes - and it does so without fuss or pretence!

From our own experience at Sanyo, there are a few regularly recurring queries that we get from our microwave customers. For example, people sometimes forget that microwave ovens are not thermostatically controlled and therefore if food is left on for too long it can ignite spontaneously, or in other words, catch fire! This is particularly so if the food has a high fat content - so watch out for sausage rolls, plum puddings, etc - our advice would be to not leave the oven unattended when such items are cooking.

On the other hand, we get people thinking there's a problem with their oven if they see steam coming out of the vents. This is quite normal, particularly where products have a high water content.

People sometimes have trouble setting the shorter cooking times accurately on ovens with manual controls. There is a little trick here - if you are setting the timer for, say $1\frac{1}{2}$ minutes, turn the dial beyond 2 and click it back to $1\frac{1}{2}$. This advice is good for all brands of mechanical control ovens. Microwaves with digital controls can, of course, be set accurately simply by keying in the cooking time.

Microwaves can interfere with TV and radio reception - especially if you are receiving an MMDS signal. Our range, like all the leading brands, complies with the highest international standards but there can still be a problem with this. The best tip is to keep the oven as far as possible away from the TV or radio.

Finally, we should just mention a couple of points that will help you make the most of your microwave. Microwave is not like conventional cooking - it's obviously much quicker but it also cooks the food in a completely different way. Because of this it is very difficult to be absolutely precise about cooking times - your own commonsense and experience of using your oven should always play an important part in planning your cooking. And lastly, we cannot over-emphasise the importance of keeping your microwave clean - it will maintain its efficiency, give you better results and help give it a longer working life.

Happy Cooking!

Mervyn Groves,

Managing Director, Sanyo Ireland.

Microwave Information and Handy Tips

1. Never turn on the microwave without having something in it – i.e., a cup of water – otherwise you will damage your microwave.

2. Read the manufacturers *Book of Instructions*.

3. Become familiar with the dials on your microwave initially by reheating and defrosting. Then try out recipes.

4. Always stir a cup of boiling water before adding tea/coffee or it will overflow due to lack of oxygen. Always taste anything reheated in a cup with a spoon as it is impossible to determine the temperature of the contents by feeling the outside of the cup. The microwaves concentrate on heating the contents of your dish/cup therefore you are able to handle the cup without the use of oven gloves.

5. Do not coat meat, chicken, etc, with beaten egg as this forms a seal like a skin and will burst.

6. Always prick the skin of tomatoes, apples, peppers and potatoes and the yolks of eggs otherwise the skin will burst and spatter the contents in the oven.

7. If you have a jar of honey which has crystallised, remove the lid, place the jar in the oven and microwave on Medium (50%) for two minutes.

8. If reheating a scone or pastry based product, place a piece of kitchen paper underneath otherwise the base will get soggy from the condensation.

9. Condensation is normal in the microwave. To eliminate it after cooking either leave the door open for a few minutes after cooking or wipe with a piece of kitchen paper.

10. When cooking fatty foods like chicken, place a sheet of kitchen paper over the breast to prevent spatters hitting the top of the oven which will require cleaning afterwards.

11. When reheating meals on plates, it is better to cover with kitchen paper, as cling film – unless vented by turning back one side – will create steam and can make your meal soggy.

12. Pyrex is ideal for using in the microwave. The lids are loose enough to allow steam to escape and the range of sizes is ideal for family meals.

13. Never use gold or silver rimmed cups/plates/dishes, etc, in the microwave as they will reflect the microwaves back into the magnetron and cause damage. The same applies to silver ties which come with freezer bags, cooking bags, etc. Also never use foil trays which come with frozen pies, apple pies, etc.

14. If you leave you cup of tea/coffee out of your hand and forget about it – reheat it for 30 seconds and it will taste exactly as it did when you made it.

15. Jelly can be dissolved without adding water. Just microwave for 45 seconds. Then you can add cold water gradually, stirring continuously thereby reducing the setting time.

16. When defrosting, leave the wrapping on the product – i.e., plastic bag. The bag will not melt.

17. You do not have to defrost peas/green beans/Brussel sprouts, etc, before cooking. You can also place the quantities you require in freezer bags with very little water and cook several types of vegetable at once. This is very convenient if you have children with different tastes, whereas before you could not cook several different vegetables in different saucepans because of lack of space on the hob.

18. When calculating times of recipes against your own wattage of your microwave, follow this simple guideline:

If your microwave is 800 watts and the recipe you are following is for 700 watts, deduct 1 minute per 100 watts.

If on the other hand the recipe is for 800 watts and your oven is 700 watts then you add a minute to the cooking time as your oven would cook slower than the 800 watt.

19. If you use cheap stewing beef with a lot of sinew it will turn out tough as the microwave will concentrate on the sinew. Trim fat and sinew off stewing beef before cooking. Remember that microwaves cook quickly so they do not have the time to soften tough pieces of meat.

20. If cooking large pieces of meat – roast beef, lamb, bacon – I would recommend the purchase of a temperature probe. This will tell you the inside temperature of the meat and you will be able to judge when it will be cooked more precisely.

21. When cooking bacon, I would recommend you cook it in a casserole dish with the lid on as bacon spatters a lot. Do not take any notice of the spattering sounds as it is only fat bursting.

22. *Browning:* As microwaves do not brown food, the following suggestions may be helpful:

a) Magic cooking bags will colour your chicken/ roast, etc.

b) Schwartz microwave seasoning can be shaken on top of the roast.

c) Paprika sprinkled on top gives a rich colour.

d) Bisto and a little water mixed to a smooth paste and brushed on works very well.

e) Soy sauce and vegetable oil or breadcrumbs sprinkled on top.

f) In the case of puddings/sponges chocolate and coffee flavours are ideal. Alternatively chocolate/ coffee toppings.

23. If your kitchen paper blows off whatever you are cooking, just wet it a little with a drop of water and this will weigh it down sufficiently.

24. When reheating a scone, 15 seconds is enough time as it has already been cooked. Remember to place the scone on a piece of kitchen paper to avoid the base going soggy.

25. Fish cooks very quickly in the microwave. A normal fillet of plaice/cod/whiting will only take two minutes, a full trout will take 4 minutes. Be careful as it is very easy to overcook fish.

26. Always cook for the least number of minutes recommended in the recipe. You can always continue to cook for another 30 seconds but it is very easy to over-cook when microwaving.

27. Herbs can be dried in the microwave. Place your herbs between two sheets of kitchen paper and micro-wave on high for three minutes or until dry and flaky. Rub the sheets of kitchen paper together and store herbs in an airtight container.

28. Flowers can also be dried in a microwave. How-ever, if you 'overcook' them, they will flake just like herbs.

29. Always keep your microwave clean otherwise the microwaves will concentrate on the dirt which will throw out your cooking times.

30. Sauces, soups, custards, etc, come out perfectly when made in a microwave. You do not get the lumps as you would on the normal hob if you do not continue to stir.

31. *Browning dish:* This is the only container which you can place in a microwave empty and turn on the microwave. Usually the browning dish is heated in the microwave for five minutes approximately. Then you remove it from the microwave. The dish will be hot so use oven gloves. The heat in the dish will brown your chops, rashers, sausages, etc, but if you want to cook six chops for example remember that the dish is cooling down while you are using it. Place the chops in the dish, wait for 30 seconds, turn and remove. Place in the second, turn and remove as above. If the dish cools down you will have to reheat it again for another 5 minutes before continuing. *However it is very important to follow the instructions given with your own type of browning dish.*

32. *Stacking frame:* This is ideal where you have two or three children arriving at one time for lunch/dinner. Stack your meals and cook them at the same time. If you find one is cooler than the others, stop half way during cooking and rotate dishes.

33. *Poached eggs:* You can get an accessory which holds water underneath and the eggs – up to five – sit in cups on top. A similar type of product was brought out previously as an attachment for a frying pan. Remember to pierce the yolks of eggs before cooking.

34. *Boiled eggs:* It is better not to try these in your microwave as you could cause damage if the egg bursts. They can be cooked on defrost for five minutes but I would not recommend it. Accessories can also be purchased for egg boiling. Personally I would stick to the hob method of boiling eggs.

35. One accessory which is very handy is the meat tray. It has slits for the meat juice to go through and the tray underneath collects the juice. Ideal for carving later or to pour the juice for using in gravy. It is also very good for cooking chicken as this contains a lot of fat.

36. Cocoa is lovely out of a microwave. Put your cocoa into your mug, add sugar, a little milk and stir until blended. Fill the mug with cold milk and microwave on high for $1^1/2$ minutes. Stop once during cooking to stir.

37. Baked potatoes are very easy in a microwave. Pierce the skin about four times with a fork [place on paper towel] and cook on high for four minutes. Two potatoes would take about six minutes, three potatoes would take about eight minutes. Try to have potatoes of an even size. Large quantities of potatoes would not save time in the microwave but ideal for small quantities. You can also cut slits on the top of the potatoes and put cheese in these. Not only do they look good but they taste great.

38. Because the microwave only uses a 13 amp plug it is very economical on electricity. The cooking time is also reduced by the cooking process and also there is no preheating with a microwave, it actually starts to cook as soon as it is turned on.

Example of cooking times:

1 large chicken – Normal oven – $1^1/2$ hours

1 large chicken – Microwave – 20 minutes

39. By using a microwave you automatically have less washing up. You can have scrambled egg, boiled milk, porridge at any time you like and you can serve in the dish which it has been cooked in. No dirty saucepans to clean. Many of the recipes can be cooked on the dish in which it is served which will cut down on wash up.

40. Circular dishes are better to use as microwaves concentrate on an angle too much thereby overcooking at the corners.

41. *Standing time:* This is important when cooking a joint of meat, turkey, large thick stew, etc.

The food continues to cook after the oven has been turned off. In the case of a large joint of meat you would require a standing time of possibly twenty minutes. You remove the meat from the microwave and cover with tin foil to retain the heat while it finishes cooking. While this is going on, take this time to cook your vegetables or dessert. You will be surprised how quickly the time goes. In the event of cooking a chicken, you will find that the time has elapsed by the time you have served the accompanying vegetables on the plates.

There is no need to think about standing time in the case of light products like eggs, fish, light puddings, custards, sauces, etc.

42. When purchasing bowls look for those which are microwave proof as there is little or no difference in the price. Everyone has plenty of suitable dishes at home for the microwave without going out especially to buy some. Be careful of using plastic and make sure the plastic you use is suitable for a microwave.

43. Bread baskets and wooden boards can be used for very short periods of time in the microwave. If used over a long period they will dry out.

44. When cooking straight from the freezer remember to defrost meat first. Also, home made pies with a large quantity of meat need to be defrosted before cooking.

45. It is better not to use salt/pepper to season prior to cooking as the taste is much stronger after microwaving. Add these after cooking.

46. Do not add too much milk when scrambling eggs. I recommend 1 tablespoon of milk per egg.

47. Rice cooks perfectly and will not stick when cooked in a microwave, but does not cook faster than the conventional method. Again no dirty saucepans.

48. Use microwave cling film only. Do not use the standard cling film. If you find that the microwave cling film tears when you try to slit it, cover the dish, then double back one edge which will suffice.

49. If you are using a combination oven/microwave remember that you cannot use plastic when operating the conventional oven. Also the dishes will get hot when using the conventional oven. Again you must be careful when using the grill and make sure you do not use a container which will melt. Pyrex is ideal in these instances. Use oven gloves.

50. Use very little water when cooking vegetables. One or two tablespoons will be sufficient. Always slit the stalk of broccoli or cauliflower before cooking to ensure even cooking. The nutrients are retained in vegetables as they are cooked quickly and you are not pouring them down the drain when straining.

51. *Turntable:* This is to distribute the microwaves evenly during cooking. Even though you have a turntable you will still have to stir the contents occasionally.

52. If you do not have a turntable you will have to stop the cooking process and rotate the dish inside. One advantage of not having a turntable is to be able to cook a leg of lamb, leg of pork or a turkey as the legs will not get caught when trying to rotate on the turntable. Again you will have to rotate to ensure even cooking.

53. *Stirrer Fan:* This is instead of a turntable. The fan rotates from the ceiling of the oven thereby circulating the microwaves.

54. *Grill:* This can be handy in a microwave but the grill element is usually 1,000 watts, sometimes 1,100 watts. The grill on a conventional cooker is 2,000 watts so it will take longer to grill something on the grill in a microwave cooker. They are ideal for colouring food which you have already microwaved.

55. Because microwaves cook much faster than the normal method of cooking, smells, as in that of cauliflower are greatly reduced.

56. Increase the juice from citrus fruits by heating for 40 seconds before squeezing.

57. Never block the vents at sides/back or top of your oven.

58. Always open lids of casseroles away from your face as steam builds up inside and could burn you.

59. Do not rinse the turntable in water straight after cooking or it could crack. Leave it stand for 20 minutes.

60. If you leave out something from the ingredients, remember to reduce your cooking time.

61. Cooking times may vary a little as the cooking times will depend on the density of the items being cooked and each oven will vary in capacity, size and wattage. You must try the recipes given and adjust accordingly. This will come with practice and time.

62. Never heat alcohol as in making a hot whiskey. You may heat the water and sugar, then add the whiskey. If you try to heat the whiskey on its own it could ignite. In some recipes you will be asked to heat alcohol for 30 seconds at the low setting. This is acceptable.

63. When making hot whiskey do not put the slice of lemon into the water when you are heating it as the taste of lemon increases to such an extent that the taste of lemon will eliminate the taste of alcohol.

64. Microwave cookers are ideal for anyone who has difficulty in bending down to take a roasting dish from the conventional oven. Being at table top height they make the transfer of dishes into and out of the oven safe and easy to handle.

65. Microwave cookers are portable. You can use them on the patio when barbecuing to reheat what has already been cooked on the barbecue or you can take them on holidays with you if you are renting a house or going to a mobile home. On holidays you do not want to have to go back to the time-consuming way of preparing a meal. Speed is of major importance.

66. When cleaning your microwave cooker abrasive cleaners are not to be used. Regular cleaning with warm water and a cloth will suffice.

67. Remember that leaded crystal cannot be used in the microwave because of the lead content.

68. Meat should be at room temperature before cooking for best results.

69. To peel tomatoes place 2 cups of boiling water in bowl or jug, add the two tomatoes and heat on high for 1 minute or until the skin splits. Plunge tomatoes into cold water and then you can peel the tomatoes easily.

70. Tear free onions. Trim the ends off the onion, place on a paper towel, heat on high for 30 seconds. Remove skin and chop/slice or whatever.

71. Refresh crackers or biscuits by placing on double layer of paper towel, cook on high for one minute, let them stand for 2–3 minutes and they will be perfectly dry and crispy again.

72. If you find there is a smell in your microwave after cooking curry, chilli, fish, etc, deodorise your oven by placing a cup of warm water with a slice or two of lemon in it into your oven and microwave for 2–3 minutes.

73. Recycled paper towels are not suitable for microwave use as there could be particles of metal contained in them.

74. Use glass containers not plastic when cooking foods which contain a high sugar content as sugar gets very hot and could melt some types of plastic.

75. You can shield food with small amounts of aluminium foil to avoid overcooking, i.e., poultry wings, turkey legs or the tail of fish.

76. If you have a combination microwave with grill and oven please use oven gloves at all times as you can easily forget that when using the grill or convection oven the dishes will get hot.

77. If you are using stock cubes just cover the cube with cold water and microwave on high for 1 minute. Stir to blend cube with water.

78. To colour chops a mixture of soy sauce and vegetable oil is a good combination. Just brush on, then microwave in the normal way.

79. If you like frozen pizzas, frozen pies, etc, a browning dish would be essential for you. You heat the browning dish first, then place the pizza on the dish and microwave for 2 minutes. This ensures that the base of the pizza does not go soggy. Remember to remove the foil dish under the pies.

80. Sliced pineapple rings (unsweetened) or corn niblets added to rice make a great salad.

81. When making jelly, add syrup from peaches/pears, etc, which you may have left over after making a flan.

82. You can not bake directly on the glass turntable, i.e., to make quiche. You must bake the pastry in another dish which is to be placed on top of the glass turntable.

83. Plates can not be heated in a microwave.

84. Unless stated – do not cover dishes in the following recipes.

85. Never use a butter carton to melt butter as the plastic is too soft and will melt.

86. Microwaves are ideal for melting butter for making stuffing. You can melt it in the dish in which you are making the stuffing.

87. *Covering food:* If you need the steam to help you cook/heat, then you cover the food, eg., vegetables, soups, casseroles. These require steam as well as microwaves to help cook and thereby reduce cooking times. Foods which are covered in breadcrumbs or which require a dry top should not be covered, eg. omelette, chicken kiev, bread and butter pudding.

88. The lids of pyrex dishes can be ideal for baking apple tarts, etc.

89. Do not use foam containers in which you get bunburgers from a take away. You can purchase special microwave proof foam containers if required.

90. If you want to tie a plastic bag an elastic band is ideal. It will not heat or cook and will be just the same as before use.

91. Cocktail sticks and wooden skewers can be used to tie a stuffed chicken, chicken kiev, cabbage rolls, or the wooden skewers can be used on the barbecue and reheated in the microwave when the guests arrive.

92. When cooking rashers use a meat rack with slits through which the fat falls. Cover with kitchen paper. Remember to snip rind with kitchen scissors to avoid curling.

93. For a simple hot syrup place 2 tablespoons of dark sugar in a bowl with 1 oz butter and cook on high for 2 minutes. Ideal topping for ice cream but remember to pour on just before serving as it will melt the ice cream.

94. Coloured kitchen paper is usually not recommended as the colours could go on food while cooking. You can use a coloured kitchen paper if you either wrap or cover food with the white side.

95. Cheese gets stringy when overcooked so remember to heat gently.

96. To reheat rice add 1 tablespoon water and cover. Cook on high for 2–3 minutes.

97. Fondue parties are made very simple with the help of your microwave. The cheese can be popped in and reheated at regular intervals.

98. To test for jam setting, place a small spoonful of jam on a saucer and allow to become cold. If it wrinkles when pushed with a finger, setting point has been reached.

99. To sterilise jars, half fill with water and heat until boiling. Pour off the water and drain for a short time before filling.

100. It is important to stir during cooking as microwaves cook from the outside in. You will see this clearly when microwaving an omelette or minced beef. As the microwaves do not cook evenly, it is important to stir food every two minutes. Remember, cooking times in the microwave are very short.

101. If you make your sauce in a measuring jug it is easy to pour.

102. To test if your favourite mug or dish is microwave proof fill the cup to one-third and heat on high for 30 seconds. If the cup/dish is cool and the water warm, it is microwave proof. If however, the water is cold and the dish is warm, it is not suitable for microwave use. Remember, microwaves cook what is in the container, not the container.

BREAKFAST

PORRIDGE

¹/₄ cup oat flakes
¹/₂ cup water
Pinch of salt

Place the oatmeal and water in a serving bowl. Cook for 1¹/₂ minutes on high. Stir once during cooking. **Do not cover.**
Milk may be used instead of water.

READYBREK

Heat required milk for 30 seconds. Add readybrek and sugar to taste. Stir and serve.

SCRAMBLED EGGS FOR TWO

4 eggs at room temperature
4 tablespoons milk
Pinch of salt
1 teaspoon butter or margarine

Melt butter in a bowl for 30 seconds. Add eggs and milk, lightly beaten together. Cook on high for 2 minutes. Stir every minute. You may need to cook for a further 30 seconds but as it is very easy to overcook eggs, cook for

the least time mentioned, then give it another 30 seconds
if required.
*To vary scrambled eggs you could add a pinch of mixed herbs
and ground black pepper or grated cheese.*

FRIED EGG

1 teaspoon margarine or butter
1 egg

Melt butter or margarine in a saucer for 30 seconds.
Remove from the microwave and break the egg onto the
melted fat. Prick the yolk with a fork (it will not run) and
microwave on high for $1^1/2$ minutes.

POACHED EGGS

600 ml boiling water [1 pint]
Pinch of salt
2 eggs

Pour boiling water into a large dish or measuring jug.
Reheat on high for 1–2 minutes until boiling. Break the
eggs onto a plate and prick the yolks with a fork and
slide them into the water. Cover with cling film or a
saucer and heat on high for 2 minutes. Leave to stand for
$1–1^1/2$ minutes until set.

Hot Grapefruit

1 grapefruit
2 teaspoons soft brown sugar
2 teaspoons sherry

Cut grapefruit in half. Separate segments. Sprinkle soft brown sugar over each half and pour sherry over each. Heat on half power (5) for 3 minutes.

Irish Breakfast

2 rashers
28 g butter (1 oz)
1 tomato halved
4 button mushrooms
1 egg
1 tablespoon milk
Salt and pepper

Snip the rind of the rashers with kitchen scissors. Place rashers on each side of the breakfast plate. Melt butter in a cup and brush on tomato halves and mushrooms. Place between ends of rashers. Add the egg and milk to the remaining butter, season and beat with a fork. Place a cup in the centre of the plate, microwave on high (10) for $2^1/_2$–3 minutes. Remove cup and whisk egg. Set aside. If you want a crisper rasher, cook for a further 30 seconds. Turn scrambled egg out onto centre of plate.

STARTERS

Corn on the Cob

4 frozen corn on the cob
56 g butter (2 oz)

Arrange in a casserole dish. Put $1/2$ oz (14 g) butter on each cob, cover with lid and microwave on high for 6 minutes. Rearrange the cobs and turn, baste with melted butter and microwave on high for a further 6 minutes. Serve topped with a little extra butter, salt and pepper.

Stuffed Mushrooms

6 large mushrooms (whole)
14 g garlic butter ($1/2$ oz)
28 g breadcrumbs (1 oz)

Remove stalks from mushrooms.

To make garlic butter see page 54.

Melt garlic butter for 20 seconds uncovered on high. Add breadcrumbs and stir. Spoon into mushrooms. Cover with microwave cling film with side turned back and cook on high for three minutes.

Salmon Stuffed Mushrooms

12 large mushrooms
6 tablespoons flaked tinned pink salmon
6 tablespoons breadcrumbs
2 teaspoons finely chopped parsley
2 teaspoons lemon juice
2 tablespoons of butter melted
Grated white cheddar cheese

Remove the stems from the mushrooms. Chop finely. In a dish, add salmon, breadcrumbs, mushroom stems, parsley and lemon juice. Melt the butter for 45 seconds and add to the above. Fill the mushrooms with the mixture. Sprinkle with the grated cheese. Arrange the mushrooms in a circle in the dish. Cover and vent and cook for 5 minutes.

Stuffed Tomatoes

4 large tomatoes about 112g (4 oz) each
2–3 small potatoes peeled and cut into small squares
1 small onion finely chopped
2 tablespoons water
224 g cottage cheese sieved (8 oz)
3 tablespoons milk
1 tablespoon chopped parsley
1 grated carrot
Salt and pepper

Slice off top of each tomato 1.2 cm/¹/₂ inch from the top. Scoop out pulp and turn tomatoes upside down to drain.

Mix potatoes, onion and water in a 1.2 litre/2 pint bowl. Cover and microwave on high (100%) for 7–10 minutes, until the potatoes are soft.

Add cottage cheese, milk, herbs, seasoning and carrot to the potato and onion and mix well. Turn tomato shells over and fill with the cheese and potato mixture. Arrange the filled tomatoes in a circle. Microwave on 100% high for 5–6 minutes or until heated through. Rotate once during cooking and at this time place top on tomatoes.

Soups

FRENCH ONION SOUP WITH CROUTONS

56 g butter (2 oz)
448 g onions sliced (1 lb)
1 litre stock/2 beef cubes (1³/₄ pints)
2 slices toast buttered
84 g grated cheddar cheese (3 oz)
3 teaspoons cornflour

Melt the butter in a large casserole dish for 1 minute on high. Toss the onions in the butter, then cook for 5 minutes.

Melt the beef cubes in a little water, stir to blend. Then add the remaining water to 1³/₄ pints [1 litre]. Add to the onions and cook on high, covered, for 10 minutes. Blend cornflour with 2–3 tablespoons of cold water and add to soup. Microwave for a further 2 minutes.

Pour into individual bowls. Use pastry cutter to cut circle shapes out of toast. Place toast rings on top of the soup and spread the grated cheddar cheese on top. Return bowls to the microwave two at a time and cook for two minutes to melt the cheese.

Other Ideas for Croutons: – Melt 2 teaspoons of butter in a dish. Add cubed white bread and cook for 4 minutes stirring every minute. Spread on kitchen paper and leave drain and stand for a further 5 minutes before putting on the soup.

Cut rings from a French stick, butter and place on top of individual servings of soup. Spread grated cheese on top and return to the microwave for 2 minutes to melt the cheese.

CREAM OF
VEGETABLE SOUP

56 g butter (2 oz)
224 g carrots peeled and finely diced (8 oz)
168 g turnip peeled and finely sliced (6 oz)
1 onion finely chopped
28 g flour (1 oz)
450 ml chicken stock [cube melted] (³/₄ pint)
300 ml milk (¹/₂ pint)
Salt and pepper
Chopped parsley and whipped cream to garnish

Melt the butter in a 1.75 litre/3 pint casserole dish for 30 seconds. Add vegetables and mix well. Cook covered on high for 8–10 minutes until the vegetables are soft. Stir twice during cooking.

Stir in the flour and stock. Microwave for 10–15 minutes. Stir in the milk and season with salt and pepper. Microwave on high for 2–3 minutes, but do not boil.

When poured into individual dishes, pour a tablespoon of cream on the soup and sprinkle with chopped parsley.

CHICKEN BROTH

2 teaspoons of butter
1 chicken carcass
1 vegetable stock cube
1 onion finely sliced
1 carrot finely diced
½ crushed clove of garlic (optional)
750 ml water (1¼ pints)

Place the vegetable stock cube in a pyrex jug with one-third of the water. Microwave on high for 1 minute. Stir and add the remaining water.

Place the butter in the casserole and microwave for 15 seconds to melt. Add the onion and carrots and microwave on high for 4 minutes. Add the chicken carcass and crushed garlic. Pour the stock over. Cover and microwave on high for 10 minutes. Remove the carcass. Serve the broth.

CAULIFLOWER AND CARROT SOUP

56 g margarine or butter (2 oz)
1 large onion finely chopped
2 level teaspoons plain flour
750 ml water and vegetable stock cube dissolved (1¼ pints)
1 small cauliflower broken into florets
2 small carrots shredded
2 tablespoons cream (30 ml)
Chopped parsley to garnish

Place the butter in a casserole dish. Microwave on high for 30 seconds to melt. Add the onion and carrot. Microwave on high for 5 minutes. Stir in flour, mix together to a roux and then gradually add the stock. Microwave on high for 4 minutes. Stop once during cooking to stir. Place the cauliflower florets in another casserole dish. Cover and microwave on high for 8 minutes. Add to the soup and cook on high for 4 minutes. Pour the mixture into the food processor/liquidiser and purée until smooth. Pour back into the casserole dish and reheat on high for 3 minutes. Pour into individual bowls and garnish with chopped fresh parsley and swirls of cream.

CREAM OF MUSHROOM SOUP

6 mushrooms
4 teaspoons butter
2 tablespoons plain flour
1½ cups milk
1 cup cream
300 ml stock [or ½ vegetable stock cube and ½ pint of water] (½ pint)
Salt and pepper

Slice and dice mushrooms. Place butter in a 2 litre/4 pint casserole dish and cook for 1 minute to melt. Add mushrooms. Cover and cook on high for 3 minutes. Stir in the flour, gradually blend in the milk, then add the stock. Cook for 5 minutes on high. Stop every 2 minutes to stir. Add cream and cook for 1½ minutes to reheat. Season with salt and pepper.

POTATO AND LEEK SOUP

448 g leeks washed and sliced thinly (1 lb)
224 g potatoes peeled and diced (8 oz)
750 ml milk (1¼ pints)
150 ml water with a vegetable stock cube dissolved (¼ pint)
Salt, pepper and paprika

Place the leeks and potato in a casserole dish. Cover with the lid and microwave on high for 10 minutes. Melt the stock cube in water and add the milk. Add to leeks and potatoes. Heat for 5 minutes on high. Add the liquid to the potatoes and leeks. Pour into the liquidiser or food processor and puree until smooth. Reheat for 2 minutes before serving. Pour into individual bowls, season with salt and pepper and sprinkle a little paprika on top to garnish.

TOMATO SOUP

6 tomatoes
1 onion finely chopped
28g butter (1 oz)
1 teaspoon sugar (5 ml)
Salt and pepper
4 tablespoons of plain flour (60 ml)
750 ml water (1¼ pints)
1 vegetable stock cube crumbled
Parsley to garnish

Peel the tomatoes *('See Tips')*. In a 2 litre/3^1/2 pint casserole dish add the sliced tomatoes, onion, celery, sugar and butter.

In a pyrex jug gradually mix the flour with 150 ml (^{1}/4 pint) of water until smooth. Add the remaining hot water. Pour into a casserole dish and add the crumbled stock cube and stir well. Cover with the lid and microwave on high for 15–20 minutes until the tomatoes are tender. Stir every 5 minutes. Pass through the sieve, then heat for a further 3 minutes. Pour into the individual bowls and garnish.

Main Courses

Mushroom and Pepper Quiche

Pastry Case

168 g plain flour (6 oz)
1/2 teaspoon salt
56 g butter or margarine (2 oz)
28 g lard or white vegetable fat (1 oz)
2–3 tablespoons cold water combined with 3 drops of yellow food colouring (optional)

Sift together flour and salt, then cut in the butter and lard until the mixture resembles fine breadcrumbs. Add water, a little at a time, stirring with a fork until the mixture starts to cling together. Form into a ball and roll on a floured surface until it is 5 cm/2 inches larger than the top of a 23 cm/9 inch flan dish.

Transfer to a dish and leave to settle in a refrigerator for 10 minutes. Trim around the edge.

Prick pastry case with a fork all around the bend of the dish, across the base and around the edge. Line the base with a double layer of kitchen paper. Microwave at high (100%) for 3 minutes. Remove kitchen paper and cook again on high (100%) for 2–3 minutes.

Quiche Filling:

1 red pepper deseeded and chopped
1 green pepper deseeded and chopped
1 onion finely chopped
6 mushrooms finely sliced
2 tomatoes sliced

1 teaspoon of oil
112 g cheddar cheese grated (4 oz)
4 eggs
150 ml of milk (¼ pint)
Salt and pepper
Pinch of oregano

Place chopped peppers, onion, mushrooms and oil in a bowl. Cover and microwave on high (100%) for 2 minutes.

Beat eggs, milk and seasoning in a 1.2 litre/2 pint casserole dish. Microwave at medium (50%) for 5–8 minutes stirring every 2 minutes.

Arrange the onions, peppers and mushrooms in the pastry case. Spread with grated cheese and pour the egg mixture over. Microwave on medium (50%) for 20 minutes. Decorate with sliced tomato sprinkled with grated cheese.

IRISH STEW

450 ml cold water (¾ pint)
4 rack chops or 448 g mutton pieces trimmed
1 large onion sliced
6 large potatoes peeled and sliced
1 large carrot sliced
3 teaspoons cornflour

Microwave chops on high for 2 minutes. Place a layer of sliced potatoes on the bottom of the casserole dish. Line with chops, next layer with onions then carrots. Season well with salt and pepper. Finally layer with sliced potatoes. Half fill the casserole with cold water. Cover with casserole lid and microwave on high for 25 minutes. Remove from the oven and add cornflour to 3 or 4 tablespoons of water and pour over the Irish stew. Return to the microwave and cook for 5 minutes. Stand for 10 minutes.

I find Irish stew very bland so if you wish to add a little extra flavour you could follow the following suggestions:

You could add a sliced parsnip and crushed clove of garlic. I would also suggest that you use a vegetable stock cube with the water for extra flavour.

PORK FILLET WITH ONIONS

2 onions cut into rings
1 cooking apple, peeled, cored and sliced
28 g butter (1 oz)
672 g pork fillet, fat removed and cut into cubes (1¹/₂ lbs)
300 ml boiling chicken stock (¹/₂ pint)
¹/₂ teaspoon oregano
1 tablespoon tomato puree
56 g button mushrooms sliced (2 oz)
3 teaspoons of cornflour
Salt and pepper

Put the onion and the apple into a 600 ml/1 pint mixing bowl. Cover with cling film and vent. Microwave on high for 2 minutes. Put the butter in a 1.2 litre/2 pint casserole dish and microwave on high for 30 seconds until the butter has melted. Stir in the meat, microwave on high for 2 minutes. Add the apple and onion mixture, stock, oregano, tomato purée, mushrooms, salt and pepper. Stir until all the ingredients are well mixed. Cover with microwave cling film and vent. Microwave on high for 17 minutes, stirring twice during cooking. Cream the cornflour with a little water and stir into the pork. Microwave on high for 1 minute and stir. Remove from the microwave, cover with tin foil and stand for 10 minutes.

Spare Ribs with Turnip

1 kg of spare ribs (2.2 lbs)
1 turnip peeled and sliced into cubes
450 ml of water (³/₄ pint)

Place the spare ribs in a casserole dish and pour water over them. Cover, and microwave on high for 10 minutes. Remove and turn the ribs upside down. Return to the casserole dish. Add the cubed turnip and cover. Microwave on high for a further 10 minutes. Stand for 4 minutes.

Stuffed Green Peppers

4 green peppers
448 g of mince (1 lb)
1 onion finely chopped

1 clove garlic
½ cup cooked rice
1 egg
1 cup tomato sauce
3 tablespoons Worcestershire sauce

Wash peppers, remove tops, seeds and plinth. Place beef and garlic in a bowl. Cook on high for 5 minutes. Stop every 2 minutes to stir. Stir in all except the cup of tomato sauce. Fill peppers with the mixture. Arrange in a circle in a round baking dish. Cover and microwave for 10 minutes. Spread the tomato sauce on top before serving. [As an alternative to tomato sauce you can add gravy.]

Serve with rice.

SHEPHERDS PIE

1 onion chopped
300 ml boiling stock [beef stock cube] (½ pint)
1–2 tablespoons of Worcestershire sauce
Pinch of nutmeg
Salt and pepper
448 g minced beef (1 lb)
1 tablespoon breadcrumbs
448 g cooked potatoes (1 lb)
28 g butter (1 oz)
1 beaten egg

Place the beef in a large casserole dish and cook for 2 minutes on high. Stir twice during cooking time. Add onion and cook for a further 2 minutes. Gradually add the stock, Worcestershire sauce, nutmeg, breadcrumbs and seasoning and microwave on high for 12–15 minutes.

Add 28 g/1 oz of cornflour creamed with a little milk to the above.

Mash the potatoes and place on top of the casserole dish. Brush with beaten egg and microwave on high for a further 5 minutes.

Crisp under a hot grill if liked.

CAPTAINS CABBAGE

6 leaves dark green cabbage
300 ml of white sauce (½ pint) – recipe on page 81
168 g breadcrumbs (6 oz)
56 g grated cheddar cheese (2 oz)

Wash the cabbage leaves and remove centre stalk and slice. Place in a casserole and cover with a lid. Cook on high for 2 minutes until the cabbage is soft.

Make white sauce. Mix the grated cheese and breadcrumbs together. Add half to white sauce.

Add the cabbage to the sauce mixture. Microwave on high for 2 minutes with the lid on the casserole. Remove from the microwave and top with remaining breadcrumb mixture. Microwave uncovered for 2 minutes. To crisp top, place under a hot grill for 1 or 2 minutes.

CABBAGE ROLLS

8 white cabbage leaves
448 g minced beef (1 lb)
1 onion chopped
70 g long grain rice cooked (2½ oz)
1 egg
pinch of salt

Sauce

392 g can of chopped tomatoes (14 oz)
2 teaspoons of soft brown sugar
Pinch of dried herbs

Cut out hard rib from each cabbage leaf.

Break off any damaged or broken leaves from the head of cabbage. Place the leaves in a shallow dish. Cover with cling film rolled back at one side and microwave on high for 3 minutes until the leaves are pliable.

Combine the sauce ingredients and set aside.

Combine the mince, onion, cooked rice, egg and salt and shape into 8 small loaves. Overlap cut edges of the leaves and put a meat loaf at the base of each leaf. Roll up. Place the rolls, seam down. Pour sauce over them and microwave on high (100%) for 8 minutes. Stand for 5 minutes.

Meat Loaf

448 g minced beef (1 lb)
84 g breadcrumbs (3 oz)
1 onion finely chopped
56 g mushrooms sliced (2 oz)
1 teaspoon dried parsley
1 tablespoon tomato ketchup
1 beef stock cube
1 egg lightly beaten
Dash Worcestershire sauce
Salt and pepper

In a large bowl mix the meat, breadcrumbs, onion, mushroom, parsley, ketchup and crumbled beef stock cube.

Mix thoroughly and bind with a beaten egg. Add the Worcestershire sauce and seasoning.

Turn mixture into a loaf dish and press down firmly.

Heat on power 7 (70%) or full for 15 minutes. Stand for 5 minutes.

Chilli Con Carne

448 g mince (1 lb)
1 finely chopped onion
Jar of chilli con carne sauce

Crumble mince into a casserole dish. Add the onion and cook for 5 minutes. Stop and stir every 2 minutes. Add a jar of chilli con carne sauce and cook for 10 minutes. Serve with rice.

For variety try adding a tin of baked beans – sauce included – to the above. This gives extra bulk and tastes great. Serve with rice or noodles.

Alternatively make your own sauce – see recipe on page 78.

GAMMON JOINT

2 kg gammon (4.4 lbs)
1 tablespoon of honey
84 g of demerara sugar mixed with 1 teaspoon of dry mustard (3 oz)
Cloves

Put the drained gammon into the roasting bag with the honey. Arrange on an upturned saucer in a round casserole dish. Slit the roasting bag at the base to enable the steam to escape and microwave on high for 10 minutes. Turn the joint over and microwave on power 8 for 25 minutes. Allow to stand, covered with tin foil for 20 minutes. Remove the gammon and peel away the skin. Score the fat into diamond shapes with a sharp knife and press the sugar and mustard mixture into the fat. Press a clove into each diamond. Place under a preheated hot grill until the gammon is crisp and brown.

If preferred, you could remove the skin and coat the gammon with toasted breadcrumbs instead of the sweet mixture.

Sausagemeat and Eggs

336 g sausagemeat (12 oz)
1 green pepper chopped
1 onion chopped
8 eggs
150 ml milk (¹/₄ pint)
84 g cheddar cheese grated (3 oz)
Salt and pepper

Put sausagemeat in a large bowl. Stir in the green peppers and onion. Microwave on high (100%) for 4 minutes until the meat is no longer pink. Stir half way through the cooking time. Pour off any excess fat. Spread in a baking dish.

Beat eggs together with milk, salt and pepper in a 2 litre bowl. Microwave on 50% (medium) for 7 minutes until the eggs are set. Stir every 2 minutes. Stir in the cheese and pour over the sausagemeat. Cover with cling film rolled back at one edge. Microwave on 50% (medium) for 10–12 minutes. Leave to stand, covered, for 5 minutes.

Chicken Kiev

4 chicken breasts
168 g butter (6 oz)
1 clove of garlic

4 tablespoons brown breadcrumbs
1 tablespoon chopped parsley
1 tablespoon paprika

Garlic butter: Place 4 oz/112g of butter in a bowl and microwave at 30% for 10 seconds. This is to soften the butter and to heat it gently. Add garlic, finely chopped or crushed and stir. Chill in the freezer for 10 minutes.

Place the chicken breasts on greaseproof paper and beat to 0.5 cm/^{1}/$_4$ inch thickness. Microwave 2 oz/56g of butter at 100% for 30 seconds or until melted. Place breadcrumbs, parsley and paprika in a bowl and mix well. Place garlic butter at the end of each chicken breast, fold the end over the butter, fold in the sides and roll up. Secure with cocktail sticks. Brush the chicken rolls with melted butter. Sprinkle with crumb mixture. Place around the edge of a round dish. Microwave on high for 7 minutes. *Do not cover.*

CHICKEN CORDON BLEU

4 chicken breasts
4 slices cooked ham
4 slices Gruyere cheese
1 egg beaten
2 slices of bread, crumbed
Paprika

Prepare as for Chicken Kiev (above). Instead of garlic butter, place the cheese rolled up in ham at the end of each chicken breast and roll up. Stand on the folded edge. Brush with beaten egg and coat with breadcrumbs. Sprinkle paprika on top. Cook in the micro-wave for 8 minutes and stand for 3 minutes.

SWEET AND SOUR CHICKEN

448 g of raw chicken meat* (1 lb)
Jar of sweet and sour sauce with chunky vegetables

* Use whatever chicken meat remains when you have removed the chicken breasts for the chicken kiev. This is ideal for the dark meat which is not as popular as the chicken breasts. The idea of this recipe is to give you an alternative to chicken curry when you have chicken left over. If using cooked chicken, cook the sauce on its own for 4 minutes, then add the chicken and cook for 1 minute. Previously cooked chicken must be gently reheated not cooked.

Place uncooked chicken in a casserole dish and cook for 4 minutes. Add the jar of sweet and sour sauce and cook for a further 2 minutes. Serve with rice.

If you prefer to make your own Sweet and Sour Sauce see recipe on page 79.

CHICKEN CASSEROLE

2 teaspoons of margarine or butter
750 g chicken pieces (1³/₄ lbs)
600 ml mushroom soup [1 pint] (see recipe page 39)

Melt the margarine or butter in a casserole dish for 45 seconds. Add the chicken pieces and coat with melted butter. Cover with the lid and microwave on high for 15 minutes. Make up the soup and pour over the chicken pieces. Microwave on high for a further 6 minutes. Stir every 2 minutes.

LASAGNE

Meat Sauce:
1 onion chopped
1 clove garlic crushed
112 g mushrooms chopped (4 oz)
2 tablespoons of oil (30 ml)
336 g minced beef (12 oz)
392 g can of tomatoes (14 oz)
$1^1/_2$ fl oz tomato puree (40 ml)
1 beef stock cube
1 teaspoon of mixed herbs

Pasta:
168 g lasagne (6 oz)
1 teaspoon of oil (5 ml)

Cheese Sauce:
42 g margarine ($1^1/_2$ oz)
42 g flour ($1^1/_2$ oz)
450 ml milk ($^3/_4$ pint)
112 g grated cheese (4 oz)

Place the onion, garlic and mushrooms in a bowl with oil. Cook for 4–5 minutes until soft. Add the remaining meat sauce ingredients. Stir well and cook for 15 minutes until cooked.

Place the lasagne in a large dish with oil. Cover with boiling water. Cook for 9 minutes until soft. Remove and drain. Melt the margarine for 1 minute. Blend in the flour and gradually add the milk. Cook for 3-4 minutes, stirring every minute until thick. Stir in half of the grated cheese. Layer first lasagne, then meat sauce, then lasagne again. Pour cheese sauce over and finish by sprinkling over the remaining grated cheese. Cook for a further 8 minutes uncovered.

Spaghetti Bolognaise

448 g minced beef (1 lb)
1 clove garlic crushed or finely chopped
1 onion finely chopped
Bolognaise sauce (recipe page 82)

Place the mince in a casserole dish and microwave on high for 3 minutes. Remove and stir. Add the chopped onion and garlic and microwave on high for 4 minutes. Stir twice during the cooking time.

Add the bolognaise sauce. Stir well and cook on high for a further 3 minutes.

Spaghetti
224 g spaghetti (8 oz)
2 teaspoons olive oil
600 ml of water (1 pint)

Place the above in a dish and cook for 7–8 minutes on high. Leave to stand in a covered dish for 5 minutes. Strain and serve under the bolognaise.

Baked Mince

448 g minced beef (1 lb)
1 onion finely chopped
1 beef stock cube
210 g can baked beans (7½ oz)
3 tablespoons of water
Salt and pepper
448 g potatoes peeled and thinly sliced (1 lb)
A little grated cheese

Place the beef and onion in a 3 pint (1.75 litre) casserole dish. Stir well and microwave on high for 3 minutes. Stir and pour off excess fat. Add the crumbled stock cube, beans and water. Stir and season with salt and pepper. Arrange the potato slices over the surface, to cover thinly. Cover with a lid and microwave on power 7 for 20 minutes. Sprinkle a little cheese over the potato and return to the microwave oven for 2 minutes on high to melt.

Steak and Kidney Pie

336 g stewing beef trimmed of fat and sinew (12 oz)
84 g beef kidney trimmed (3 oz)

1 beef stock cube
28 g plain flour (1 oz)
Salt and pepper
1 onion finely chopped
75 ml water (3 fl oz)

Pastry
112 g self-raising flour (4 oz)
56 g suet (2 oz)
Salt
30 ml/2 tablespoons water
1 egg beaten

Cut beef and kidney into cubes. Crumble beef cube into the flour. Season with salt and pepper and mix well. Toss meat into the flour. Place in a pyrex bowl. Mix in the onion and water gradually.

Cook on high for 6 minutes. Stir, then cover with the lid. Heat on power 4 (medium) for 12 minutes. Stir, re-cover and at this stage add pastry on top of the beef. Cook again on power 4 (medium) for a further 12 minutes. Stand for 5 minutes before serving.

Pastry:
Combine flour, suet and salt in bowl. Mix in water and beaten egg to form a soft dough. Pat or roll out to the diameter of the casserole dish and place on top of the meat.

QUICK POTATO PIE

2 tablespoons butter
1 onion finely chopped

448 g cold roast lamb/beef/chicken/turkey/pork (1 lb)
2 tablespoons chopped parsley
250 g cooked peas (9 ozs)
250 g cooked carrots sliced (9 oz)
250 g fresh mushrooms (9 oz)
1 teaspoon curry powder
300 ml mushroom soup – (¹/₂ pint) see recipe page 39
448 g mashed potatoes – previously cooked (1 lb)
Paprika

Melt the butter in a casserole dish for 30 seconds. Add the onion and cook for 2 minutes on high. Toss in the meat, parsley, peas, carrots, mushrooms, curry powder and soup.

Top with mashed potato. Sprinkle with paprika and cook on high for 15 minutes.

Pepper Omelette

4 eggs
2 tablespoons of milk
Salt and pepper
Knob of butter
¹/₄ of a green pepper seeded and chopped
¹/₄ of a red pepper seeded and chopped
¹/₂ small onion finely chopped

Place peppers and onions in a bowl with butter and microwave on high for 2 minutes. Beat the eggs and milk together. Melt a little butter in a casserole dish. Pour the egg mixture into a dish. Cook uncovered on high for 3–4 minutes. Lift the edge all round to make sure any uncooked mixture goes to the base of the casserole dish. Cook on high for 2–3 minutes.

Place the cooked peppers and onions over half of the omelette and fold the uncovered half over. Serve immediately.

LAMBS LIVER WITH MUSHROOMS AND ONIONS

448 g lambs liver (1 lb)
1 level teaspoon flour
56 g butter or margarine (2 oz)
448 g onions finely chopped (1 lb)
4 streaky rashers rindless and chopped
112 g mushrooms sliced (4 oz)
15 ml – 1 tablespoon wine vinegar

Cut the liver into thick slices and toss in the flour. Preheat a large browning dish according to the manufacturers instructions. Add 28 g (1 oz) of butter for the last minute. Place the liver in the hot butter and microwave on high for 5 minutes. Turn the slices after 3 minutes. Remove to the preheated dish. Cover.

Add the remaining butter to the cooking dish and microwave on high for 1 minute until melted. Stir in the onions, bacon and mushrooms into the butter. Cover and cook on high for 5 minutes. Stir frequently. Stir in the vinegar and the liver. Cook on high for 2 minutes. Stir and serve.

Beef Casserole

1 tablespoon vegetable oil
1 onion peeled and sliced
3 celery sticks trimmed, washed and chopped
1 clove garlic crushed or finely chopped
56 g lean streaky bacon rindless and diced (2 oz)
1 level teaspoon of flour
2 level teaspoons of curry powder
448 g lean minced beef (1 lb)
1 level teaspoon of tomato puree
224 g can of tomatoes (8 ozs)
Salt and pepper
150 ml natural yogurt (¼ pt)

Put the oil in a large casserole dish with celery, garlic and bacon. Cover with the lid and cook on high for 5–7 minutes. Stir in the flour and curry powder. Microwave on high for 2 minutes. Stir in the minced beef, tomato purée and can of tomatoes. Cover and microwave on high for 20 minutes. Stir every 3–4 minutes. Gradually add the yogurt and microwave on high for 2 minutes. Stand for 5 minutes.

Serve with rice or garlic bread.

FISH

Easy Fish

1 fish fillet (cod, plaice, etc.)
2 slices lemon

Place fish on serving plate and top with lemon slices.
Cook on high for 2 minutes. Check, and a further 30
seconds may be required depending on the size of the
fillet.

Flake the edge of the fish with a fork to test. If the
fish flakes away, the cooking is finished. Ideally you
could have cooked broccoli for the first five minutes
alone then added the fish for the remaining two minutes.

Fresh Trout and Vegetables

1 green pepper sliced in rings
1 red pepper sliced in rings
2 tablespoons of water
1 lemon sliced
1 teaspoon margarine
1 medium trout cleaned and head removed

Melt the margarine in a dish for 30 seconds. Place the
pepper rings in rows and cook for two minutes on high.
Place the trout on top and pour the water over. Cover
with cling film venting one side to allow the steam to
escape. Cook for 4 minutes on high. Depending on the
size of the trout, you may need to cook for a little longer.
Cook for 30 seconds at a time. You will know when the

trout is cooked by flaking the sides of the fish with a fork. If the fish flakes, stop the cooking process. Serve with a wedge of lemon.

SALMON STEAKS

2 salmon steaks
2 teaspoons lemon juice
1 tablespoon parsley chopped
2 teaspoons butter

Melt the butter for 30 seconds on high and brush on both sides of the salmon. Place in a casserole dish. Pour lemon juice over the steaks. Cook uncovered in the microwave for 6 minutes. Remove from the microwave and brush with melted butter. Sprinkle with parsley.

HADDOCK IN WHITE ONION SAUCE

448 g of haddock (1 lb)
300 ml cold water (½ pint)
28 g butter or margarine (1 oz)
2 tablespoons plain flour
300 ml milk (½ pint)
Salt and pepper

Place the haddock in a casserole dish and pour the water over. Cover and cook for 2 minutes on high. Stand for 1 minute and then pour the water off.

Melt the butter in a measuring jug for 30 seconds on high. Add the onion – chopped – and cook for 2 minutes. Add the flour and stir. Blend in the milk slowly. Microwave on high for 3 minutes stirring every 1¹/₂ minutes. Pour over haddock and continue to cook for 2 minutes.

FISH PIE

672 g cod fillet (1¹/₂ lbs)
84 g butter or margarine (3 oz)
300 ml of milk (¹/₂ pint)
Salt and pepper
672 g potatoes peeled and sliced [or previously cooked] (1¹/₂ lbs)
1 egg beaten
28 g flour (1 oz)
3 eggs hard boiled and sliced
56 g shelled prawns (2 ozs)
1 teaspoon chopped parsley

Put the cod into a casserole dish, and dot with 28 g (1 oz) of butter. Add 150 ml (¹/₄ pint) of milk. Season well with salt and pepper. Cover with the lid or microwave cling film turned back at one edge to vent. Microwave on high for 5 minutes. Strain the juices from the cod into a measuring jug and make up to 300 ml (¹/₂ pint) with milk. Flake the cod. If the potatoes need to be cooked put them in a large casserole dish with a teaspoon of water, cover and microwave on high for 12–15 minutes, until cooked. Stir twice during cooking. Drain and mash with 28 g (1 oz) of butter and beaten egg.

Put the remaining 28 g (1 oz) of butter in an oven proof bowl and microwave on high for 30 seconds until melted. Stir in the flour and mix to a roux. Gradually add in the measured milk. Microwave on high for 45 seconds, then whisk. Microwave on high for $1^1/_2$–2 minutes until boiling. Whisk every 30 seconds. Season well with salt and pepper.

Fold the flaked cod, prawns and eggs into the sauce. Pour into a large casserole dish. Spoon the mashed potatoes on top of the fish. Microwave on high – uncovered – for 8 minutes. Sprinkle with chopped parsley and serve.

Smoked Kippers

Place two kippers on a plate and cover with damp kitchen paper. Cook on high for 2 minutes and serve. This could also be used a starter.

Plaice in White Sauce

448 g plaice (1 lb)
300 ml white sauce (¹/₂ pint) [page 81]
Juice of ¹/₂ a lemon

Make up a white sauce. Add lemon juice. Put the plaice in the casserole dish and cook uncovered for 4 minutes on high. Turn once during cooking. Pour sauce over and cook on high for a further 2 minutes.

COD WITH LEEK AND CORN STUFFING

1 leek washed and trimmed
42 g butter (1½ oz)
56 g white breadcrumbs (2 oz)
42 g cheddar cheese grated (1½ oz)
1 x 326 g can of sweetcorn (11½ oz)
Salt and pepper
2 tomatoes skinned (see 'Tips')
1 egg beaten
4 cod steaks (168 g/6 oz each)

Slice the leek and place in a bowl with 2 tablespoons of salted water. Cover and cook for 4 minutes. Melt the butter in a dish for 45 seconds, add the leek to the breadcrumbs, cheese, seasoning and sweetcorn. Reserve 2 tablespoons of sweetcorn for garnish.

Chop one tomato and add to the mixture. Bind the stuffing with the beaten egg. Wash and trim the fish. Place in a large casserole, cover and cook on high for 5 minutes. Stand for 5 minutes. Stuff the cavity of each cod steak with the stuffing mixture. Also cover the end of each steak with the mixture. Cover and cook for 3 minutes. Turn and cook for a further 3 minutes.

Garnish with sliced tomato and the remaining corn.

Mussels in Garlic Breadcrumbs

Note: *When buying fresh mussels check that shells are shut tight. Discard any open ones. Scrub the shells under cold running water. Soak for 1–2 hours before use.*

224 g mussels (8 oz)
3 fl oz water (75 ml)
28 g garlic butter (1 oz) see recipe page 54
28 g brown breadcrumbs (1 oz)
14 g butter (^{1}/₂ oz)

Place the mussels in a 2 litre/3^1/₂ pint casserole dish, cover and microwave on high for 2–3 minutes. Stir once during cooking time. At the end of cooking, all shells should be open; discard any mussels which remain closed.

Melt the garlic butter in a bowl by microwaving for 45 seconds. Mix in the breadcrumbs and stir. Melt the butter in a small bowl. Add the mussels and make sure that all are coated in melted butter. Get a small amount of garlic breadcrumbs in a spoon and cover each mussel and replace on the lid of the casserole dish. When all mussels have been coated in garlic breadcrumbs, cook uncovered on high for 4 minutes.

VEGETABLES

French Potatoes

672 g potatoes, peeled and very thinly sliced (1½ lbs)
1 medium sized onion, sliced into rings
42 g butter (1½ oz)
Salt and pepper
6 tablespoons of milk
Paprika

Soak the potato slices in cold water. Put the onion rings in a bowl. Cover with cling film and vent. Microwave on high for 1 minute. Grease a 2 pint (1.2 litre) casserole dish with a little of the butter. Layer the drained potatoes and onions in the dish, starting and finishing with the potatoes. Season each layer well with salt and pepper. Pour the milk over the potatoes and dot with the rest of the butter. Sprinkle the top with paprika. Cover with cling film and vent. Microwave on high for 13 minutes. Stand for 5 minutes before serving.

Stuffed Baked Potatoes

2 large potatoes about 224 g each (8 oz)
28 g butter or margarine (1 oz)
1 small onion, skinned and finely chopped
2 tablespoons of milk
84 g cheddar cheese grated (3 oz)
2 tablespoons of chopped parsley
Salt and pepper

Scrub the potatoes thoroughly, then pierce them all over using a fork. Microwave on high for 10 minutes or until soft. Place the butter in a medium bowl and microwave on high for 30 seconds or until melted. Add the onion and mix thoroughly. Three-quarters cover with cling film and microwave on high for 3 minutes or until the onion is soft. Halve the potatoes and scoop out the insides, leaving a thin shell. Add the potato flesh to the onion and mash well together. Add the milk, half of the cheese and the parsley. Season to taste. Mix well together. Pile the mixture back into the potato shells and place them on a large ovenproof serving dish. Sprinkle with the remaining cheese and microwave on high for 2 minutes or until heated through.

COLCANNON

448 g potatoes sliced (1 lb)
28 g of butter or margarine (1 oz)
28 g chopped onion (1 oz)
224 g cabbage chopped (¹/₂ lb)
Salt and pepper
¹/₂ cup of milk

To cook potatoes and cabbage:
Peel and slice the potatoes and place them in a casserole dish. Wash and remove the centre stalk from the cabbage leaves and chop them roughly. Make a well in the centre of the potatoes and place the cabbage inside. Pour water over. Cover and cook on high for 10–12 minutes until the potatoes are soft. Remove the lid and drain. Leave the lid off for a few minutes to dry out the potatoes. Mash the potatoes and cabbage together.

In a separate bowl, melt the butter for 30 seconds and add the chopped onion. Cook at 50% (half power) for 2 minutes. Add to the mashed potatoes and cabbage. Gradually add the milk and stir well.

Cover and cook for a further five minutes uncovered.

Ratatouille

1 onion sliced
1 green pepper – plinth and seeds removed
1 red pepper – plinth and seeds removed
1 zucchini/courgette sliced (if available)
2 tomatoes chopped
1 aubergine sliced (if available)
6 large mushrooms – sliced
1 clove of garlic crushed or sliced very finely

If you are omitting any of the ingredients just add one extra vegetable to balance the timing.

Combine all ingredients in a shallow dish. Cover and cook on high for 10 minutes.

Cauliflower and Broccoli

1 whole cauliflower
Broccoli florets
Chopped parsley

Remove outer leaves and stalk of cauliflower. Place the cauliflower in a large casserole dish. Cover and cook on high for 5 minutes. Add broccoli florets around the head of the cauliflower. Cover the casserole and continue cooking for a further 6 minutes.

Sprinkle with chopped parsley and serve.

Carrots and Cauliflower

1 head cauliflower
6 carrots

Slice carrots. Break up the florets of the cauliflower.

Place in the casserole dish with 4 tablespoons of water and cover.

Cook on high for 10 minutes.

Parsley Potatoes

4 medium potatoes peeled
1 teaspoon butter melted
1 tablespoon fresh chopped parsley

Cut the potatoes into 1 cm/^{1}/$_2$ inch slices. Layer in a shallow dish. Cover and cook on high for 8 minutes. Uncover and drain. Pour melted butter over and sprinkle with parsley. Cook on high for 3 minutes.

Sauces

CHILLI CON CARNE SAUCE

2 teaspoons chilli powder (or more if preferred)
56 g demerara sugar (2 oz)
1 teaspoon salt
1 teaspoon paprika
1 tablespoon tomato puree
3 tablespoons Worcestershire sauce
300 ml of water ($\frac{1}{2}$ pint)
2 tablespoons vinegar
2 tablespoons lemon juice
1 tablespoon cornflour
1 small tin red kidney beans

Blend all the above ingredients together and heat on high in a covered dish for 5 minutes.

This sauce is ideal if you prefer to make your own sauce rather than purchasing a prepared jar of sauce.

MUSHROOM SAUCE

28 g butter or margarine (1 oz)
28 g plain flour (1 oz)
4 mushrooms finely chopped
300 ml of milk ($\frac{1}{2}$ pint)

Place butter in a 600 ml/1 pint jug. Microwave on high for 30 seconds or until the butter has melted. Add chopped mushrooms and cook on high for 2 minutes. Add the flour and mix to roux. Gradually add the milk stirring all the time. Microwave on high for 5 minutes stirring every 2 minutes.

Sweet and Sour Sauce

¹/₂ cup brown sugar
¹/₂ cup vinegar
3–4 cups pineapple chunks and juice, unsweetened
1–2 tablespoons soy sauce
2 tablespoons oil
1 clove of garlic chopped finely
¹/₄ cup sliced mushrooms
2 tablespoons cornflour blended with ¹/₂ cup of water

Heat the oil in a casserole dish or a measuring jug for 2 minutes. Add the mushrooms and cook on high for 1 minute. Add all the other ingredients and cook on high for 5 minutes. Stir once during cooking.

The above sauce is ideal with chicken pieces, pork pieces or with beef. Also try with left over bacon.

Onion Sauce

28 g butter or margarine (1 oz)
28 g plain flour (1 oz)
300 ml milk (¹/₂ pint)
1 small onion finely chopped

Place the butter in a 600 ml/1 pint jug. Microwave on high for 30 seconds or until the butter has melted. Add the chopped onion and cook on high for 2 minutes. Add the flour and mix to a roux. Gradually add the milk, stirring all the time. Microwave on high for 5 minutes, stirring every 2 minutes.

Parsley Sauce

28 g butter or plain margarine (1 oz)
28 g plain flour (1 oz)
300 ml milk (1/2 pint)
2 tablespoons chopped parsley

Place the butter in a 600 ml/1 pint jug. Microwave on high for 30 seconds or until the butter has melted. Stir in the flour and mix to a roux. Blend in the milk gradually until smooth. Microwave on high for 5 minutes, stirring every 2 minutes, until the sauce is thick and smooth. Add the chopped parsley and stir.

Cheese Sauce

28 g butter or margarine (1 oz)
28 g plain flour (1 oz)
84 g grated cheddar cheese (3 oz)
300 ml milk (1/2 pint)

Place the butter in a 600 ml/1 pint jug. Microwave on high for 30 seconds or until the butter has melted. Stir in the flour and mix to a roux. Blend in the milk gradually until smooth. Microwave on high for 5 minutes, stirring every 2 minutes, until the sauce is thick and smooth. Add the grated cheese and stir into the sauce.

Basic White Sauce

28 g butter or margarine (1 oz)
28 g plain flour (1 oz)
300 ml milk (¹/₂ pint)

Place the butter in a 600 ml/1 pint jug. Microwave on high for 30 seconds or until melted. Stir in the flour and mix to a roux. Blend in the milk gradually until smooth. Microwave on high for 5 minutes, stirring every 2 minutes, until the sauce is thick and smooth. Season with salt and pepper.

Curry Sauce

28 g butter (1 oz)
28 g plain flour (1 oz)
1 teaspoon curry powder
1 tablespoon wine vinegar
Salt and pepper
300 ml milk (¹/₂ pint)

Place the butter in 1³/₄ pint (1 litre) jug and microwave on high for 30 seconds. Add the flour, curry powder, wine vinegar and salt and pepper. Gradually stir in the milk. Microwave on high for 3 minutes until the sauce rises to the top of the jug. Remove from the oven and beat well with a whisk.

Apple Sauce

1 large cooking apple
2 tablespoons water

Peel and slice the apple. Place in a dish, cover and vent. Cook on high for two minutes. Remove, cover and mash with a fork.

Bolognaise Sauce

28 g butter (1 oz)
3 tablespoons vegetable oil (45 ml)
1 small onion finely chopped
1 small carrot peeled and finely chopped
1 small celery stick trimmed and finely chopped
1 clove garlic crushed
1 level teaspoon tomato puree
1 level teaspoon oregano
150 ml dry red wine (¼ pint)
150 ml beef stock [1 cube dissolved] (¼ pint)
Salt and pepper

Put the butter and oil in a casserole dish and microwave on high for 1 minute. Stir in the vegetables and garlic. Mix well. Cover the dish with the lid. Microwave on high for 7–8 minutes until the vegetables begin to soften. Stir twice during cooking. Add the tomato purée and microwave on high for 3 minutes. Add the wine and stock and stir well. Cover and microwave on high for 4–5 minutes until boiling. Continue to cook on high for 10–12 minutes until the sauce is thick. Stir every 3 minutes.

CHOCOLATE SAUCE

112 g plain chocolate broken into squares (4 oz)
28 g butter (1 oz)
150 ml water or milk (¼ pint)
1½ teaspoons cornflour

Put the chocolate, butter and water/milk into a 1 litre/1¾ pint jug and microwave on power 7 (medium) for 3½ minutes. Put the cornflour in a 1.2 litre (2 pint) bowl and mix to a smooth paste with a little water. Pour the hot chocolate mixture onto the cornflour stirring all the time. Return to the microwave and cook on high for 1 minute before serving. The sauce can be served hot or cold over fruit, sponge puddings or ice cream.

CUSTARD SAUCE

2 tablespoons custard powder
600 ml milk (1 pint)
2 tablespoons sugar

Cream the custard powder with a little milk in a 1¾ pint (1 litre) bowl. Pour the remaining milk into a 1 litre (1¾ pint) jug and microwave on high for 2 minutes. Pour warmed milk onto mixed custard powder. Stir well and return to the jug. Microwave on high for 3 – 4 minutes. Stop twice during cooking and stir. Beat in the sugar until it has dissolved. Beat well with whisk and serve.

DESSERTS

Egg Flip
4 Servings

6 fresh egg yolks
56 g sugar (2 oz)
100 ml sweet dessert wine/sherry (4 fl oz)

In a small bowl whisk together egg yolks and sugar until you obtain a dense cream. Pour wine over and whisk to combine. Cook uncovered for 30 seconds at 100%. Whisk cream until soft and frothy. Repeat operation (30 seconds and whisk) three more times, that is, all in all, 2 minutes at 100%.

Pour into desert cups and serve hot or cold.

Quick Chocolate Fudge

448 g sifted icing sugar (1 lb)
56 g cocoa powder (2 oz)
Pinch of salt
3 tablespoons milk
1 tablespoon vanilla essence
112 g butter (4 oz)

Place the icing sugar, cocoa, salt, milk and vanilla essence in a large heat-proof bowl and mix together thoroughly. The mixture should still be very dry. Make a well in the centre of the dry ingredients and place the butter in one piece in the middle. Cook for 2 minutes, then stir vigorously until smooth. Pour into a small, greased and greaseproof paper lined, shallow square container. Mark into squares and leave until set.

Makes 36 squares. Power setting full.

RICH CHOCOLATE MOUSSE

224 g plain chocolate broken into squares (8 oz)
4 large eggs separated

Decoration
150 ml whipped cream (¹/₄ pint)
Grated chocolate

Place the chocolate in a 3 pint (1.75 litre) bowl and microwave on medium (power 4 or 40%) until melted – approximately 2 minutes. Stir twice during this time.

Beat yolks, one at a time into the chocolate. Whisk egg whites until they stand in soft peaks. Fold into chocolate mixture using a metal spoon.

Divide the mixture between 4 dessert dishes and chill in the fridge for approximately 1 hour to set.

Decorate with whipped cream and grated chocolate.

CREME CARAMEL

112 g caster sugar (4 oz)
75 ml cold water (3 fl oz)
1 tablespoon boiling water

3 eggs
150 ml milk (¹/₄ pint)
150 ml cream (¹/₄ pint)
Vanilla Essence

Place 84 g (3 oz) of sugar in a large bowl with cold water. Microwave on high (100%) for 3 minutes and then stir. Microwave at 100% for 7–10 minutes until the mixture is golden brown. Stir in the boiling water and let it cool slightly. Divide between four ramekin dishes.

Beat the eggs, sugar, cream, milk and vanilla essence together lightly, then strain into ramekins.

Arrange the filled dishes in a circle in the microwave and cook at medium (50%) for 5–7 minutes until the mixture is just starting to set in the centre. Remove from the cooker and allow to cool. Keep in the fridge until it is set. When turning out creme caramels, dip the base into a bowl of boiling water until it is warm to the touch. This will loosen the caramel layer.

APPLE CRUMBLE WITH COCONUT TOPPING

6 cooking apples peeled and sliced
¹/₂ a cup water
¹/₂ a cup sugar
¹/₂ a teaspoon cinnamon
70 g soft butter (2¹/₂ oz)
¹/₂ a cup coconut
¹/₂ a cup brown sugar
¹/₂ a cup flour

Place the apples, water, sugar and cinnamon in a 1 litre/1³/₄ pint casserole dish. Cover it and cook for 5 minutes on high. Rub the butter into the flour, coconut and brown sugar, and sprinkle over apples. Top with extra cinnamon and cook for 3 to 4 minutes.

Bananas in Syrup

4 bananas, peeled and sliced thickly
28 g butter (1 oz)
1 tablespoon brown sugar

Place the butter and sugar in a bowl and cook on high for 1 minute.

Add slices of banana and cook for a further 4 minutes until the bananas are opaque. Serve with whipped cream.

To serve the above as a formal dessert, add a tablespoon of brandy for the last 30 seconds of cooking time.

Basic Sponge Pudding

56 g soft margarine (2 oz)
1 egg beaten
112 g self-raising flour (4 oz)
4 level tablespoons cocoa powder
56 g caster sugar (2 oz)
Vanilla flavouring
4 tablespoons milk
1 tablespoons hot water

Beat together the margarine, sugar, egg, vanilla flavouring and the flour. Blend the hot water and cocoa together and add to the mixture. Gradually add to the milk to give a soft dripping consistency. Spoon into a greased 600 ml/1 pint pudding basin and level the surface. Microwave on low for 7–9 minutes or until the top of the sponge mixture is only slightly moist and a wooden cocktail stick inserted in the centre comes out clean. Leave to stand for 5 minutes before turning out on a heated serving dish.

Mocha Sauce
56 g plain chocolate (2 oz)
150 ml hot black coffee (¹/₄ pint)
150 ml milk (¹/₄ pint)
2 teaspoons cornflour
3 tablespoons sugar

Break the chocolate into pieces. Microwave at 50% (medium) for 3 minutes. Stir in the coffee. Gradually blend in the milk into the cornflour and stir into the sauce. Microwave on 100% for 2¹/₂–3 minutes until boiling. Stir twice during cooking. Stir in the sugar.

Pour over the upturned pudding and serve hot.

CHILLED
CHOCOLATE CAKE

224 g plain chocolate (8 oz)
112 g butter (4 oz)
2 eggs
28 g caster sugar (1 oz)
224 g digestive biscuits (8 oz)

1 teaspoon rum essence (5 ml)

Break up the chocolate and put the pieces in a small bowl with the butter. Melt in the microwave for 2–3 minutes. Mix well. Beat the eggs with the sugar until thick and creamy. Gradually add the chocolate mixture, beating well. Add the rum essence.

Break the biscuits into small pieces but do not crush completely. Fold into the chocolate mixture. Spoon the mixture into a 6 inch (15 cm) loose bottomed cake tin. Chill in the fridge overnight. Remove the cake from the tin and decorate as desired before serving. This is a very popular birthday treat.

As an alternative to using digestive biscuits, I would suggest you try peanuts or marshmallows.

Apple Bread Pudding

224 g bread broken into small pieces (8 oz)
200 ml milk (8 fl oz)
28 g butter (1 oz)
56 g soft brown sugar (2 oz)
1 egg
2 teaspoons mixed spice
56 g mixed peel (2 oz)
168 g mixed dried fruit (6 oz)
1 cooking apple
Demerara sugar

Lightly grease a 8 inch (20 cm) flan dish and line the base with greased greaseproof paper. Place the bread in a large bowl, soak with the milk and beat thoroughly until smooth. Add the butter, sugar, spice and egg and mix thoroughly. Stir in the dried fruit. Spoon the pudding into the prepared dish and cook on 50% for 10–12 minutes. Rest for 5 minutes. Peel, core and slice the apple. Place apple slices on top of the pudding while it is resting. Cook pudding for a further 10 minutes and sprinkle with demerara sugar when cooked.

STUFFED BAKED APPLES

2 medium sized cooking apples
Brown sugar
Sultanas
Lemon juice
4 teaspoons of golden syrup (20 ml)

Core the apples but do not peel. Pierce the skin with a cocktail stick several times. Place in a suitable cooking/ serving dish and fill the centre of each apple with a mixture of sugar, sultanas and lemon juice. Pour 2 teaspoons of golden syrup over each apple. Cover the fruit with greased, greaseproof paper and cook for 4–5 minutes. (4 apples would take 6-8 minutes.)

STEWED APPLE AND CUSTARD

4 large cooking apples
2 tablespoons sugar

300 ml of water (¹/₂ pint)

Peel and slice the apples. Place in a casserole dish and add water. Cover and cook on high for 4 minutes. Remove the lid, add the sugar, stir and re-cover. Microwave on high for a further minute. Remove and stir well.

Custard
1 tablespoon custard powder
1 tablespoon sugar
450 ml of milk (³/₄ pint)

Place the milk in a pyrex jug and heat for 2 minutes on high. While this is cooking, blend the custard powder, sugar and 2 tablespoons of milk together. When blended, add to the warmed milk and stir. Return to the microwave – do not cover. Microwave on high for 1¹/₂–2 minutes. Stop and stir twice during cooking time.

Rice Pudding

56 g pudding rice (2 oz)
28 g caster sugar (1 oz)
28 g butter (1 oz)
600 ml milk (1 pint)
1 teaspoon ground nutmeg (5 ml)

Place the rice, sugar, butter and milk in a 2 pint (1.2 litre) dish and stir. Leave the dish uncovered and bring to boiling point on 100% for 7–10 minutes, stirring every 5 minutes. Reduce to 50% and cook for a further 20 minutes, stirring every 5 minutes. Sprinkle with ground nutmeg.

Bread and Butter Pudding

2 eggs
2 teaspoons of sugar
300 ml milk (½ pint)
3 large slices bread buttered
56 g sultanas (2 oz)
1 tablespoon of brown sugar as a topping

Cut bread into slices and arrange in a casserole dish, with sultanas in between the layers. Beat the eggs with a fork and add the white sugar and milk. Pour the beaten mixture over the bread. Allow to stand for 30 minutes to soak. Microwave on high for 5 minutes. Stand for 3 minutes. Do not cover while cooking. Sprinkle dark brown sugar on top and continue to cook for a further 4 minutes.

Golden Baked Apples

4 large cooking apples
4 teaspoon mincemeat
½ teaspoon mixed spice
4 tablespoon pure orange juice
4 dessertspoons of honey

Core the apples and then use a small piece of core to fill the base of each apple. Half way down each apple make a very shallow cut all the way around. Mix the mincemeat with the spice and use this to fill each apple cavity. Place the apples in a shallow dish. Pour the dessertspoon of honey over each one. Pour the orange juice into the base of an ovenproof dish. Cover with cling film and cook on high for 7–10 minutes. Stand for 3 minutes. Spoon the orange juice over the apples before serving with ice cream.

Pudding with Jam Topping

Oil for greasing
3 tablespoons raspberry jam
168 g self-raising flour (6 oz)
84 g shredded suet (3 oz)
84 g caster sugar (3 oz)
2 large eggs
5 tablespoons of milk

Lightly brush a 1^1/$_2$ pint (900 ml) pudding basin with a little oil. Spread the jam over the base and the sides of the pudding bowl. Sift the flour into a 3 pint (1.75 litre) mixing bowl. Mix in the sugar and suet. Beat together the eggs and milk and stir into the dry ingredients. Mix to combine. Pile into the prepared pudding basin and level the top. Microwave on medium (4) for 12 minutes. The top should still be moist. Allow to stand, covered, for 6 minutes before turning out. Serve with custard (see recipe page 83).

BREAD
PRODUCTS

Garlic Bread

1 French stick
1/2 cup butter
1 clove garlic

Soften the butter at 30% (low) for 20 seconds. Add the chopped/crushed garlic and stir. Chill in the freezer for 10 minutes.

Slice the French stick almost through the crust with 5 cm/2 inch spaces. Spread the garlic butter between the slices. Place the kitchen paper underneath the French stick and one sheet on top. Microwave on high for 2 minutes. Serve hot.

Raisin Tea Bread

84 g raisins (3 oz)
1 teaspoon bicarbonate of soda
168 g soft light brown sugar (6 oz)
Grated zest 1 orange
50 ml vegetable oil (2 fl oz)
1 egg
168 g plain flour (6 oz)
1 teaspoon ground cinnamon
1/2 teaspoon grated nutmeg
Pinch of ground cloves

Mix the raisins, bicarbonate of soda and 6 fl oz of boiling water in a bowl and leave to stand for 10 minutes until the raisins have plumped up. Mix the sugar, orange zest, oil and eggs together until smooth and add the raisin mixture. Gradually stir in the remaining ingredients. Line the base of the dish with either greaseproof paper or microwave cling film. Then pour the mixture evenly into it. Microwave at 50% (medium) for 8 minutes. Increase the power to 100% (high) and microwave for 3–6 minutes or until no uncooked mixture is visible through the base of the dish. Stand for 10 minutes.

Wholewheat Banana Bread

84 g wholewheat flour (3 oz)
84 g plain flour (3 oz)
168 g caster sugar (6 oz)
5 tablespoons vegetable oil
2 tablespoons milk
2 eggs
2 very ripe bananas sliced
1 tablespoon lemon juice
1/2 teaspoon bicarbonate of soda
Salt
56 g chopped nuts (2 oz)

Topping
56 g flour (2 oz)
56 g soft light brown sugar (2 oz)
Pinch cinnamon
28 g butter (1 oz)

Prepare the topping by mixing all the ingredients together and rub to fine breadcrumbs. Set aside.

Place the bread ingredients in a large mixing bowl and beat at low speed for 30 seconds. Line the base of a baking dish with greaseproof paper or cling film. Spread the mixture evenly in the dish and sprinkle the topping on top. Protect the ends with 5 cm/2 inch wide strips of foil. Microwave on 50% (medium) for 9 minutes. Increase to 100% and cook for 4 minutes.

Remove the foil after 2 minutes at increased power. Stand for 5–10 minutes.

SHORTCRUST PASTRY CASE

84 g of butter or margarine (3 oz)
168 g of plain flour (6 oz)
¹/₂ teaspoon salt
3 tablespoons cold water

Cut the butter into the flour and salt until the mixture is like breadcrumbs. Sprinkle with water, whilst stirring with a fork, until the mixture forms a ball. You may not need to use all the water. Form into a ball on a floured surface. Flatten to a thickness of 1.2 cm/half an inch. Roll out into a circle ·5 cm/one-eighth of an inch thick and 5 cm/2 inches larger than the top of the dish. Transfer the rolled out pastry circle to the pie dish by folding it in half, then in again. Carefully lift onto the dish without tearing. Unfold the pastry and fit it loosely into the dish. Lift the sides and let them fall gently into the dish to leave out any air pockets. Leave the pastry to relax in the fridge for 10 minutes to prevent it shrinking while cooking. Trim the pastry overhanging. Prick the pastry case continuously at the bend of the dish with a fork. Then make pricks on the bottom and sides of the pastry to ensure even cooking in the microwave. Cover the base of the pastry case with 2 layers of absorbent paper cut to size. These will absorb the steam produced during cooking and help to make the pastry crisp. Place the dish on an upturned plate in the microwave cooker. Microwave at 100% for 3 minutes. Remove the paper and microwave for 2–3 minutes. Check readiness before minimum time by looking through the base – it should appear opaque.

CHOCOLATE
ALMOND FLAN

56 g caster sugar (2 oz)
84 g butter (3 oz)
2 egg yolks
140 g plain flour (5 oz)
56 g ground almonds (2 oz)

Filling
6 teaspoons cornflour
1 tablespoon plain flour
450 ml milk (³/₄ pint)
2 teaspoons instant coffee granules
168 g plain chocolate broken into pieces (6 oz)
2 eggs
2 tablespoons orange flavoured liqueur

To finish
150 ml of cream (¹/₄ pint)
1 oz flaked almonds toasted (28 g)

1 oz flaked almonds toasted (28 g)

Cream the sugar and butter until light and fluffy. Beat in the egg yolks, one at a time, then gradually work in the flour and ground almonds to form a soft dough. Knead lightly on a floured surface. Grease a 22.8 cm/9 inch round flan dish, then roll out the pastry to fit. Chill for half an hour. Prick thoroughly to stop it from puffing up. Microwave at 100% (high) for 5 minutes until the pastry begins to colour. Allow it to cool.

Blend the cornflour, flour, milk and instant coffee together in a 2 litre/$3^1/2$ pint bowl. Add chocolate.

Microwave at 100% (high) for $5^1/2$–6 minutes or until thick. Stir vigorously every 2 minutes.

Lightly beat the eggs in a separate bowl and mix in 6 tablespoons of the hot custard. Blend, then stir into the remaining custard. Microwave at 100% (high) for about 1 minute until thick. Beat in the liqueur. Cover and chill.

About $1^1/2$ hours before serving, beat the custard until smooth and spoon into the pastry case.

Whip the cream until thick then pipe rosettes over the custard. Decorate the rosettes with toasted almonds, then chill for at least one hour before serving.

James

Raspberry Jam

896 g fresh picked raspberries (2 lbs)
448 g caster sugar (1 lb)

Place the raspberries in a 2.25-2.75 litre (4-5 pints) mixing bowl and crush them with the back of a wooden spoon. Add the sugar, cover the bowl with plastic wrap and leave in a cool place overnight. Pierce the cling film. Microwave on high for 5 minutes and stir. Microwave on power 7 for 25 minutes, stirring twice during cooking. To test for setting: put a little jam onto a cold saucer. Allow to cool for a minute or two and then push the jam with your finger. If the jam is ready, it will crinkle slightly. Pot in sterilised jars, seal and cover.
See 'Tips' for instructions on sterilising jars.

Lemon Curd

336 g caster sugar (12 oz)
168 g unsalted butter cut into cubes (6 oz)
Juice and rind of 5 lemons
6 eggs beaten and strained through a sieve

Put the sugar, lemon rind and juice into a large casserole dish and cook on high for 4 minutes. Stir well. Add butter to the mixture and cook on high for 3 minutes. Stir well and stand for four minutes. Beat the eggs gradually into the mixture. Whisk well. Cook on high for 5 minutes until the mixture is boiling, then whisk until the mixture thickens. Pour into a cold casserole dish and whisk until cool. Pour into sterilised jars.

Strawberry Jam

1 kg strawberries (2 lbs)
1 tablespoon lemon juice
1 teaspoon butter
1 kg caster sugar (2 lbs)

Place the strawberries, lemon juice and butter in a 2 litre/3¹/₂ pint casserole dish. Cover with a lid. Heat on high for 10 minutes, stir in a third of the sugar and mix until well dissolved. Cook on high for a further 3 minutes. Stir in the remaining sugar and cook on medium for 6 minutes. Stop and stir. Cook on medium for a further 10 minutes. Stand for 5 minutes. Pour into warmed sterilised jars and cool. Then cover.

Apple Chutney

1 kg cooking apples (2 lbs)
448 g onions peeled and chopped (1 lb)
168 g demerara sugar (6 oz)
300 ml of vinegar (¹/₂ pt)
Rind and juice of a lemon
100 g sultanas (4 oz)

Peel, core and finely slice the apples. Place in a pyrex bowl with the chopped onions, demerara sugar and 150 ml (¹/₄ pint) of vinegar. Cover with cling film vented and cook on high for 6 minutes. Stir. Add the remaining ingredients. Heat on high for 10 minutes. Stir and cook again on high for 10 minutes. Stir and cook finally for a further 8 minutes. Pour into sterilised jars. Leave to cool and then cover.

HOT DRINKS

Irish Coffee

150 ml water (¹/₄ pint)
1 teaspoon sugar
1¹/₂ teaspoons instant coffee
2 teaspoons whipped cream
3 tablespoons Irish whiskey

Bring the water to the boil in the glass. Add the sugar and stir until melted. Add the instant coffee and stir well. Add the whiskey and stir. Add the whipped cream gradually by running the spoon along the rim of the glass.

Decorate with a few coffee granules on top of the cream.

French Coffee

Same as above but substitute brandy instead of the Irish whiskey.

Russian Coffee

Same as above but substitute vodka instead of the Irish whiskey.

Tia Maria Coffee

Same as above but substitute Tia Maria instead of the Irish whiskey.

Mulled Wine

1 bottle red wine
$1/3$ bottle of water
1 cup orange juice
1 cup port
1 cup sugar
$1/2$ level teaspoon ground cloves
2 cinnamon sticks
1 lemon sliced

Combine all the ingredients except the lemon slices. Microwave on high for 12–14 minutes or until it is steaming. Garnish with sliced lemon.

Cooking Charts
Vegetables

Vegetable	Amount	Cooking Time	Standing Time	Method
Asparagus	448 g/1 lb	7-8 mins	2 mins	covered dish – add 30 ml/2 tbs water
Broad Beans	448 g/1 lb	12 mins	2 mins	covered dish – add 60 ml/4 tbs water
French Beans	448 g/1 lb whole beans	8 mins	2 mins	covered dish – add 60 ml/4 tbs water
Runner Beans	448 g/1 lb sliced	7 mins	2 mins	covered dish – add 60 ml/4 tbs water
Broccoli	448 g/1 lb	9-10 mins	4 mins	covered dish – add 60 ml/4 tbs water
Cabbage	448 g/1 lb shredded	9–11 mins	4 mins	covered dish – add 45 ml/3 tbs water
Carrots	448 g/1 lb cut into 1.5 cm/^{1}/$_2$ in slices	9–10 mins	2 mins	covered dish – add 30 ml/2 tbs water
Cauliflower	448 g/1 lb broken into pieces	9–11 mins	2 mins	covered dish – add 60 ml/4 tbs water
Courgettes	448 g/1 lb sliced	4 mins	6 mins	cooking bag – add 28 g/1 oz butter

Vegetable	Amount	Cooking Time	Standing Time	Method
Leeks	448 g/1 lb sliced	8–9 mins	2 mins	covered dish – add 28 g/1 oz butter
Mushrooms	224 g/8 oz	3 mins	2 mins	covered shallow dish – add 28g/1 oz butter and dash of lemon
Onions	224 g/8 oz	4 mins	2 mins	covered dish
Parsnips	448 g/1 lb sliced	8–10 mins	2 mins	covered dish add boiling, 45 ml/3 tbs water
Peas	448 g/1 lb	6–8 mins	2 mins	cooking bag – add 45 ml/3 tbs water
Potatoes boiled	448 g/1 lb even sizes	10–12 mins	3 mins	covered dish – add 60 ml/4 tbs water; serve with butter
mashed	448 g/1 lb cut into small pieces	9–10 mins	3 mins	covered dish – add 60 ml/4 tbs water; add a little butter 3 tbs milk season well and mash
baked	2 potatoes 168 g/6 oz each	6 mins	4 mins	prick with fork 4/5 times and put on kitchen paper
Spinach	448 g/1 lb	6–7 mins	2 mins	covered dish
Swede turnip	448 g/1 lb – cubed	10–12 mins	2 mins	covered dish, add 45 ml/3 tbs water

Poultry

Type	Weight	Cooking Time	Standing Time	Method
Chicken portions	per 448 g/1 lb	7 mins	3 mins	season with chicken seasoning; place thin area towards centre and cover
Turkey	per 448 g/1 lb	12 mins per 448 g power 7	20 minutes covered in foil	brush with melted butter; sprinkle with seasoning; cover with bag or cling film; turn over and around 4 times basting well during cooking; shield wings and legs with foil
Roast Chicken/ Duck	per 448 g/1 lb	7 mins per 448 g	5 mins	as above when stuffing bird allow 5 mins extra
Boneless Roast Turkey	per 448 g/1 lb	12 mins per 448 g	15 mins covered in foil	put on plate; cover with cling film or see Hints and Tips on colour. Rotate twice during cooking

Meat

Type	Weight	Condition	Full Power	Half Power
Beef	below 1 kg/2 lb	rare	first 3 mins	7–8 mins per 448 g/1 lb
-	over 1 kg/2 lb	medium	first 6 mins	8–9 per 448 g/1 lb
-	–	well done	–	9-10 mins per 448 g/1 lb
Lamb	1 kg/2 lb (+ over)	well done	first 5 mins	9 mins per 448 g/1 lb
Veal	1 kg/2 lb (+ over)	well done	first 5 mins	9 mins per 448 g/1 lb
Pork	1 kg/2 lb (+ over)	well done	first 8 mins	10 mins per 448 g/1 lb

Any meat over 2 lbs use temperature probe

Rice

Type	Amount	Cooking Time	Standing Time	Method
long grain	224 g/ 8 oz	10–12 mins	3–4 mins	covered dish; add 900 ml/1^1/$_2$ pints cold water
brown	224 g/ 8 oz	20 mins full 8 mins half	3–4 mins	covered dish; add 900 ml/1^1/$_2$ pints boiling salted water
easy cook	224 g/8 oz	10 mins	3–4 mins	covered dish; add 600 ml/1 pint boiling salted water

Pasta

Type	Amount	Cooking Time	Standing Time	Method
spaghetti	224 g/8 oz	12 mins	3–4 mins	covered dish, 1.2 litres/2 pints boiling salted water and 15 ml/1 tbs oil
macaroni	224 g/8 oz	9 mins	3–4 mins	covered dish; 1.2 litres/2 pints boiling salted water and 15 ml/1 tbs oil
tagliatelli	224 g/8 oz	6 mins	3–4 mins	covered dish; 1.2 litres/2 pints boiling salted water and 15 ml/1 tbs oil
pasta shells	224 g/8 oz	8 mins	5–6 mins	covered dish; 1.2 litres/2 pints boiling salted water and 15 ml/1 tbs oil
lasagne	6-8 sheets	10 mins	5 mins	covered dish; 600–900 ml/1–1$^1/_2$ pints boiling salted water and 15 ml/1 tbs oil

Defrosting Chart

Type	Quantity	Method	Defrost time	Standing time
chicken drumsticks	4	place thin parts towards centre of dish	6 mins	5 mins
portions	2x224g/8 oz	turn over half-way	6 mins	5 mins
whole	per 448 g/1 lb	turn half-way	17 mins	10 mins
turkey whole	per 448 g/1 lb [max 4.5 kg/10 lb]	turn over and around 4 times while defrosting	6 mins	20 mins
duck	per 448 g/1 lb	turn at halfway	17 mins	20 mins
joint	per 448 g/1 lb [max 3.6 kg/4 lb]	place on plate	15 mins per 448 g	15 mins
steak	2x224 g/8 oz	turn over half-way	8–9 mins	5 mins
lamb chop	2x168 g/6 oz	turn over half-way	4 mins	1 min
pork chop	2x196 g/7 oz	turn over half-way	6–7	5 mins
bacon [rashers]	224 g/8 oz	separate slices	3 mins	
liver lambs/pig	224 g/8 oz	separate slices	5 mins	3 mins
kidney lambs	4	turn over half-way	3–4 mins	5 mins
mince beef	448 g/1 lb	break up meat halfway	15 mins	5 mins
beefburger	2		2 mins	
Sausage meat	224 g/8 oz	break up half-way	5 mins	2 mins
casserole	672 g/1¹/₂lb	separate with fork half-way	10 mins	10 mins

Index

Tin foil, 13, 22
Tomatoes, 21, 33
Tomato soup, 40
Trout, 15
Trout and vegetables, 64
Turntable, 19, 23

Vegetables: [see veg.
    charts] 111, 112
– broccoli, 19, 74
– Brussel sprouts, 13
– Cabbage, 24, 49, 50
– Carrots and cauliflower,
    75
– Cauliflower, 19, 74
– Cauliflower and
    broccoli, 74

– Colcannon, 73
– French potatoes, 72
– Green beans, 13
– Onions, 21, 36, 79
– Parsley potatoes, 75
– Potatoes, baked, 17
– Peas, 13
– Ratatouille, 74
– Stuffed baked potatoes,
    72

Whiting, 15
Whiskey, 20
Wholewheat banana
    bread, 99
Wine, mulled, 109
Wooden skewers, 23, 24

The Irish Cookbook

Carla Blake

Traditional Irish dishes are slightly adapted here to suit present day tastes and methods and included are some modern Irish recipes using Guinness, Irish Whiskey, Irish Hams and Irish Cheese.

All the basic methods for making soup and cooking fish, meat and vegetables are given with a selection of unusual recipes. Suggestions are also made about accompaniments to make a pleasantly balanced meal. There are recipes to see you through all occasions from family meals and 'Quick and Easy' snacks to dinner parties.

Writing simply and clearly the author avoids the use of French culinary terms which often confuse the inexperienced cook. Recipes are given in ounces and grammes.

Cooking Irish Style

Noreen Kinney

In *Cooking Irish Style* Noreen Kinney brings good cooking into everyone's reach without additional expense and extra work in the process. Noreen includes several traditional dishes as well as many original ones incorporating characeristic Irish flavours. Some of the recipes included in this easy-to-follow book are:

Gammon of the Emerald Isle
Corned Beef and Cabbage
Blarney Salmon
Tripe and Onions
Irish Stew
The Leprechaun's Dainty Dish (using offals)

Noreen also shows us an alternative to smoked salmon and has very appetising recipes for Pâte, Scallops, Haddock and many other types of fish. There is also a delightful variety of recipes for soups, meat, chicken, salads and desserts.